My Coloring Book`s Volume 1

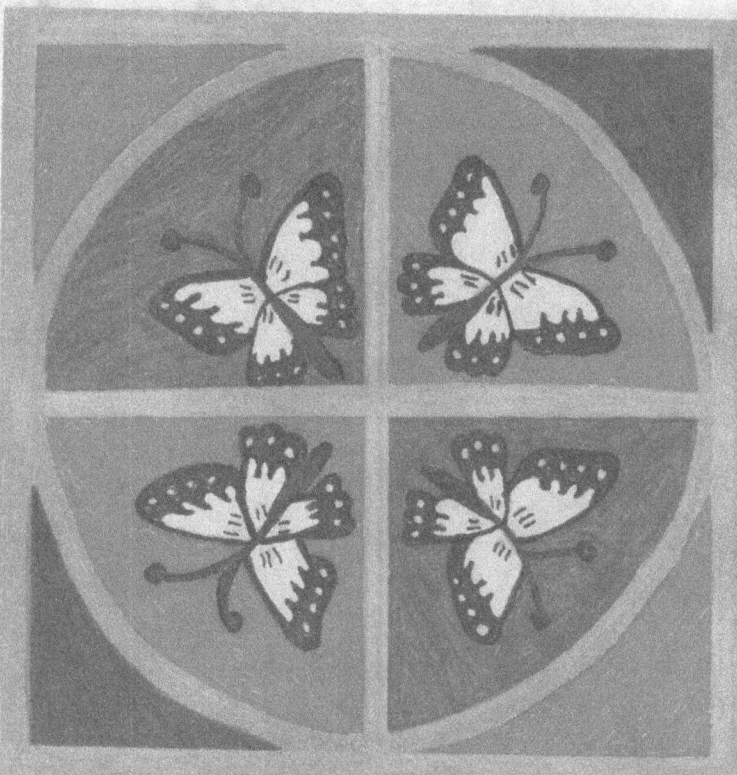

Christine Hardy

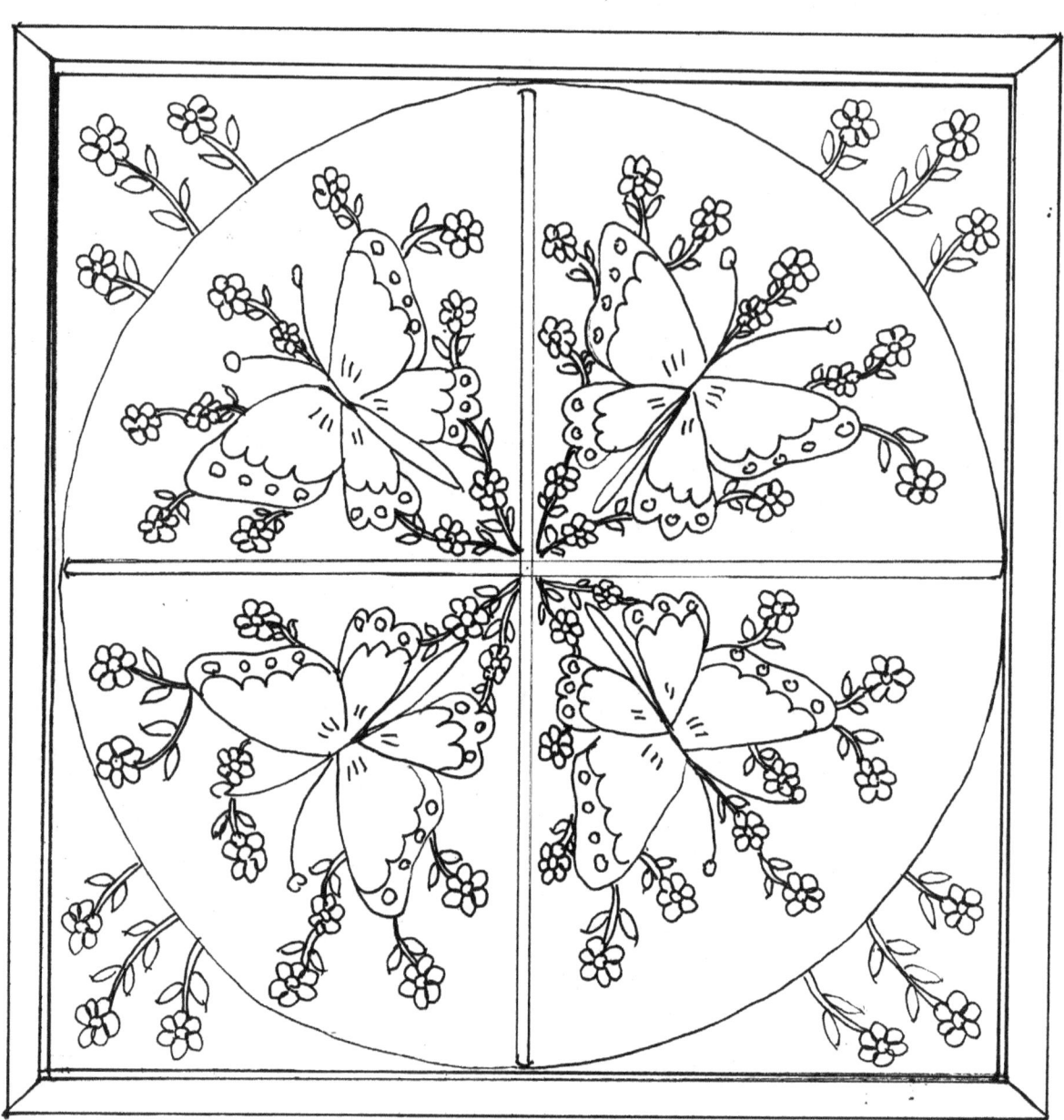

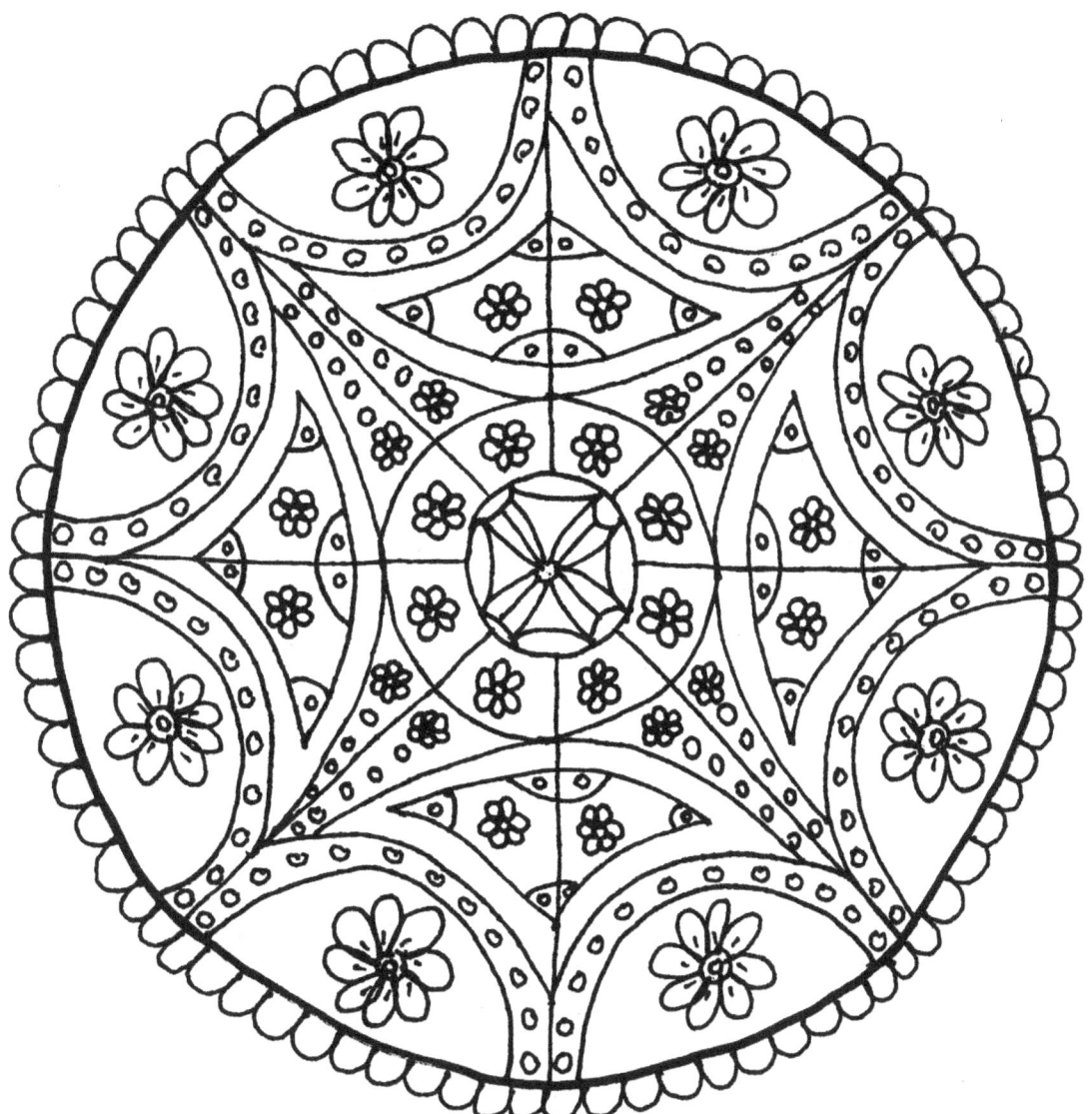

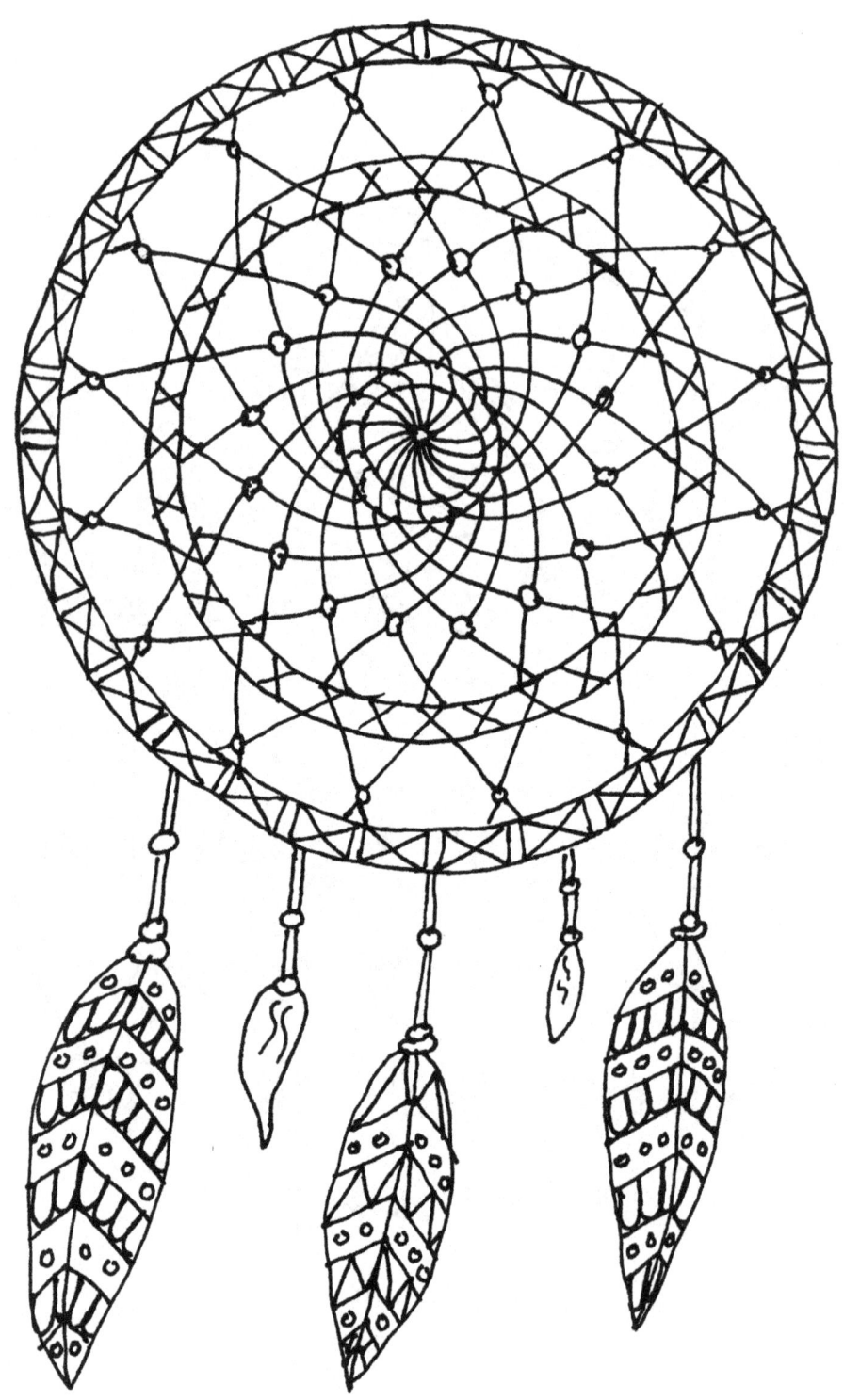

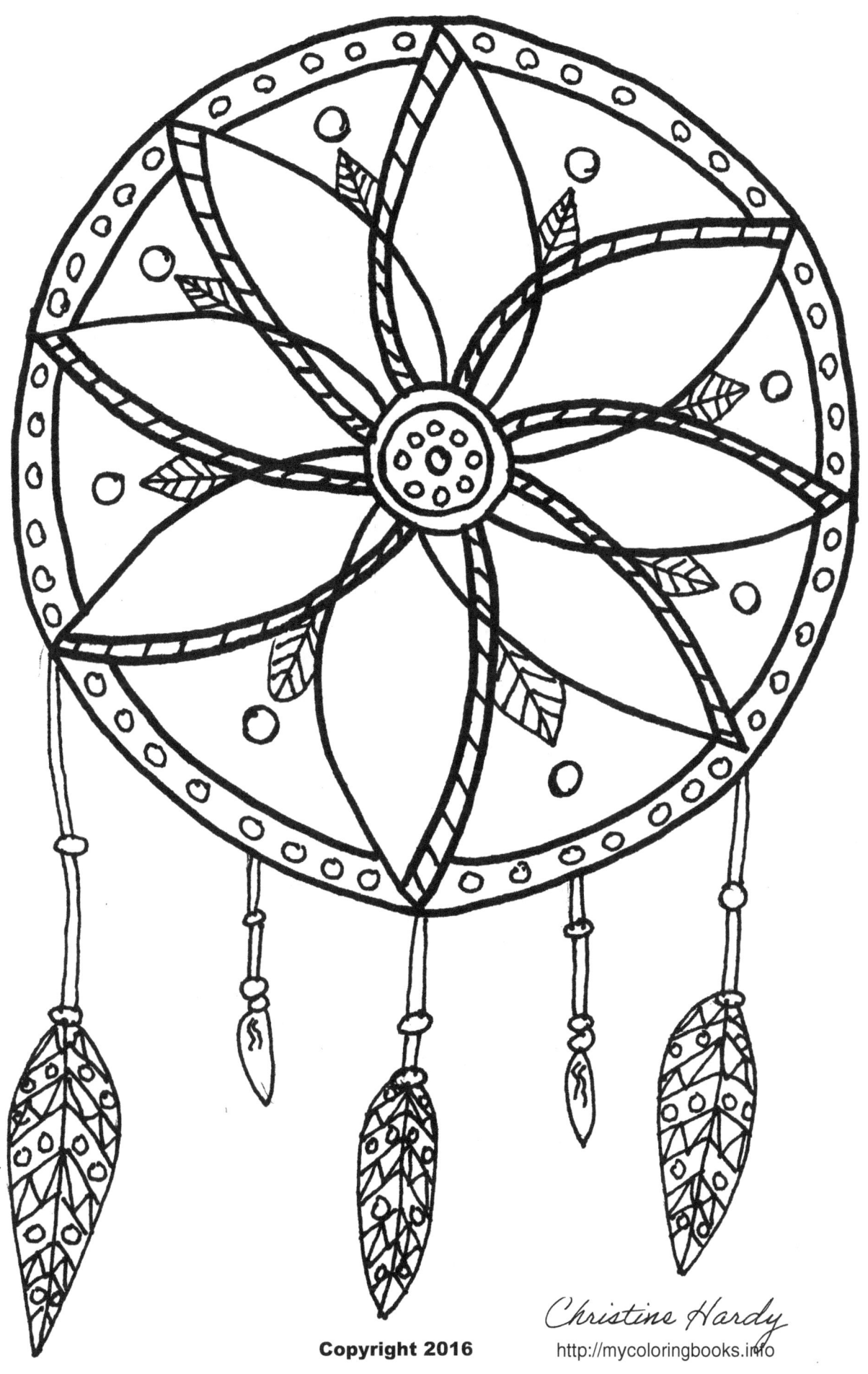

Christine Hardy

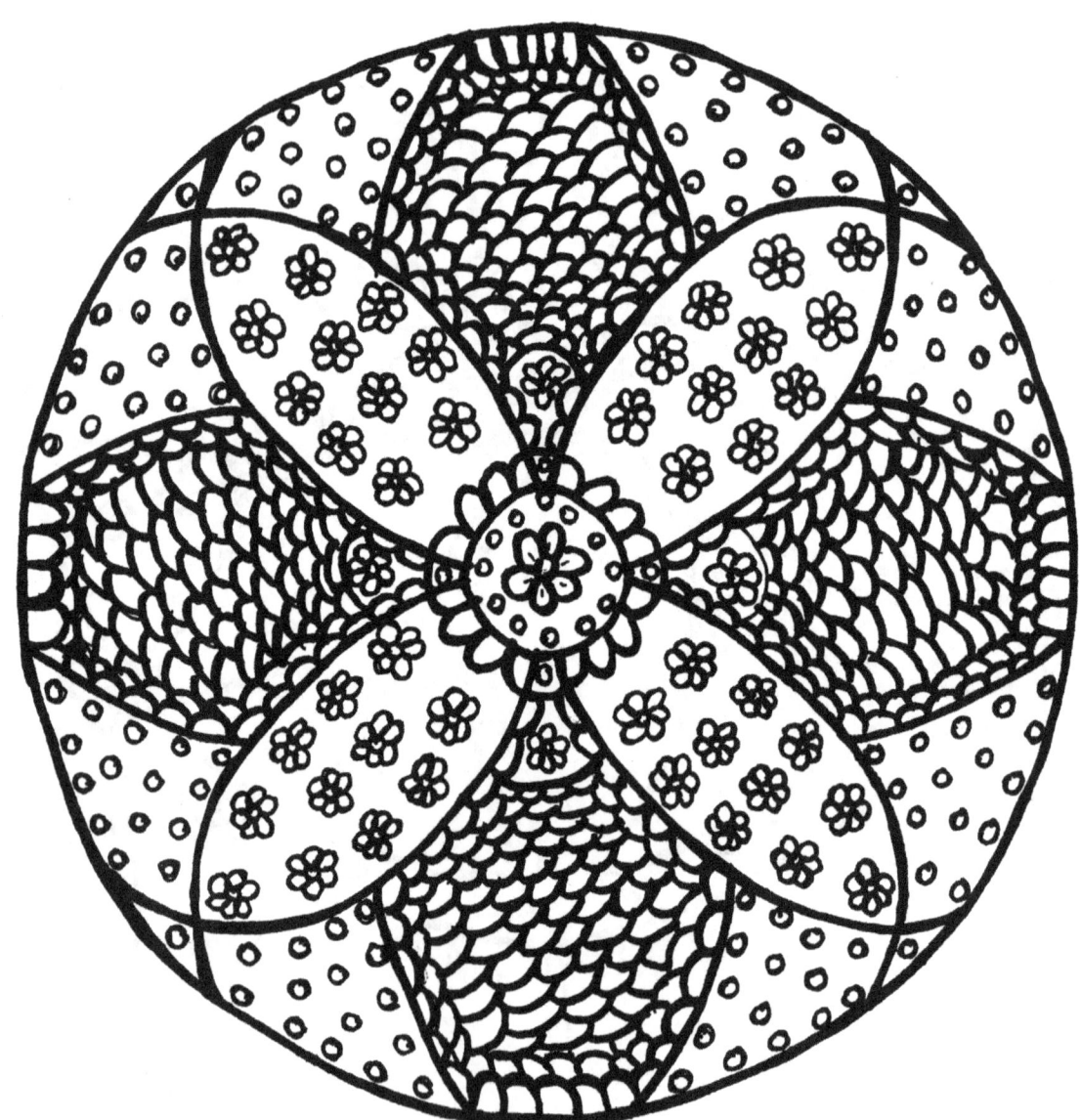

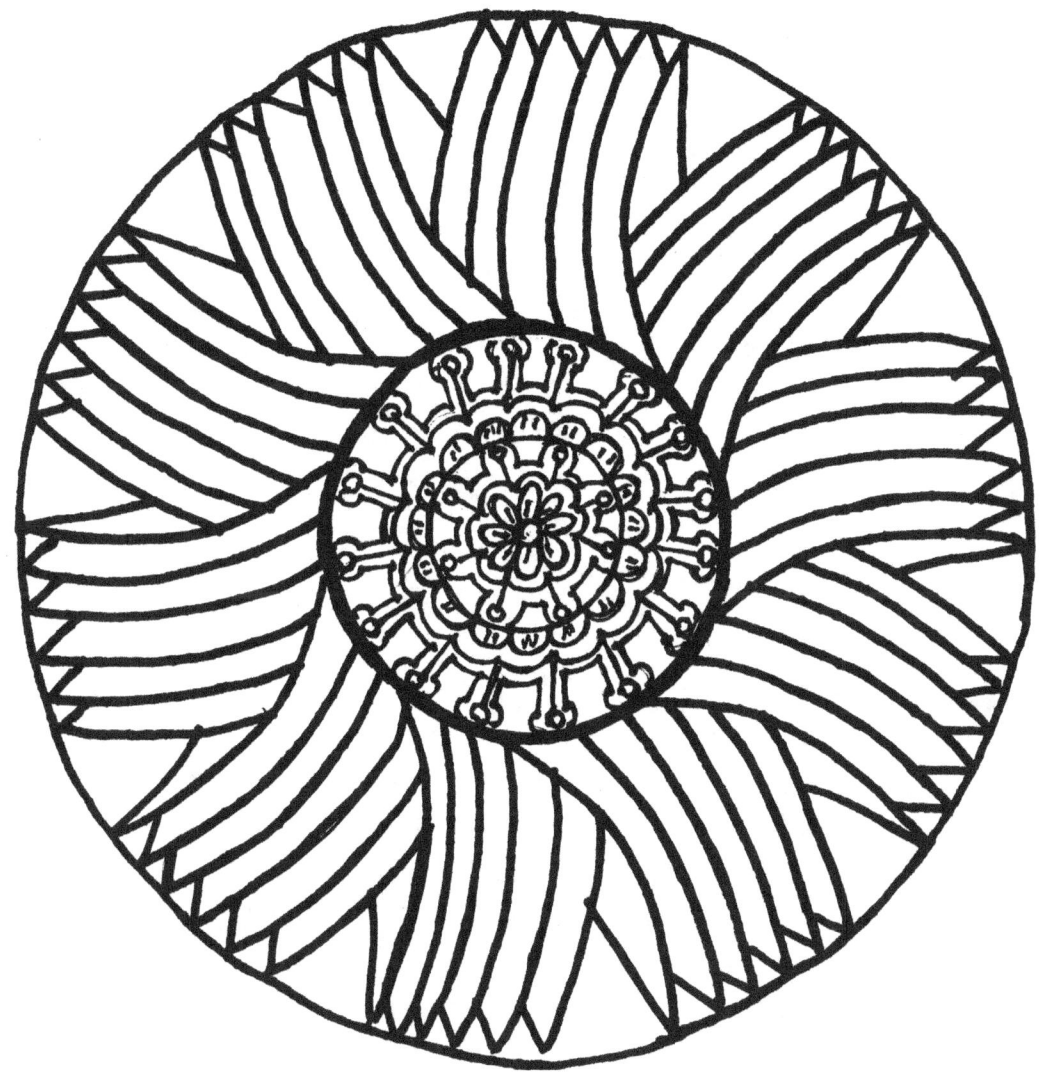

Copyright 2016

Christine Hardy

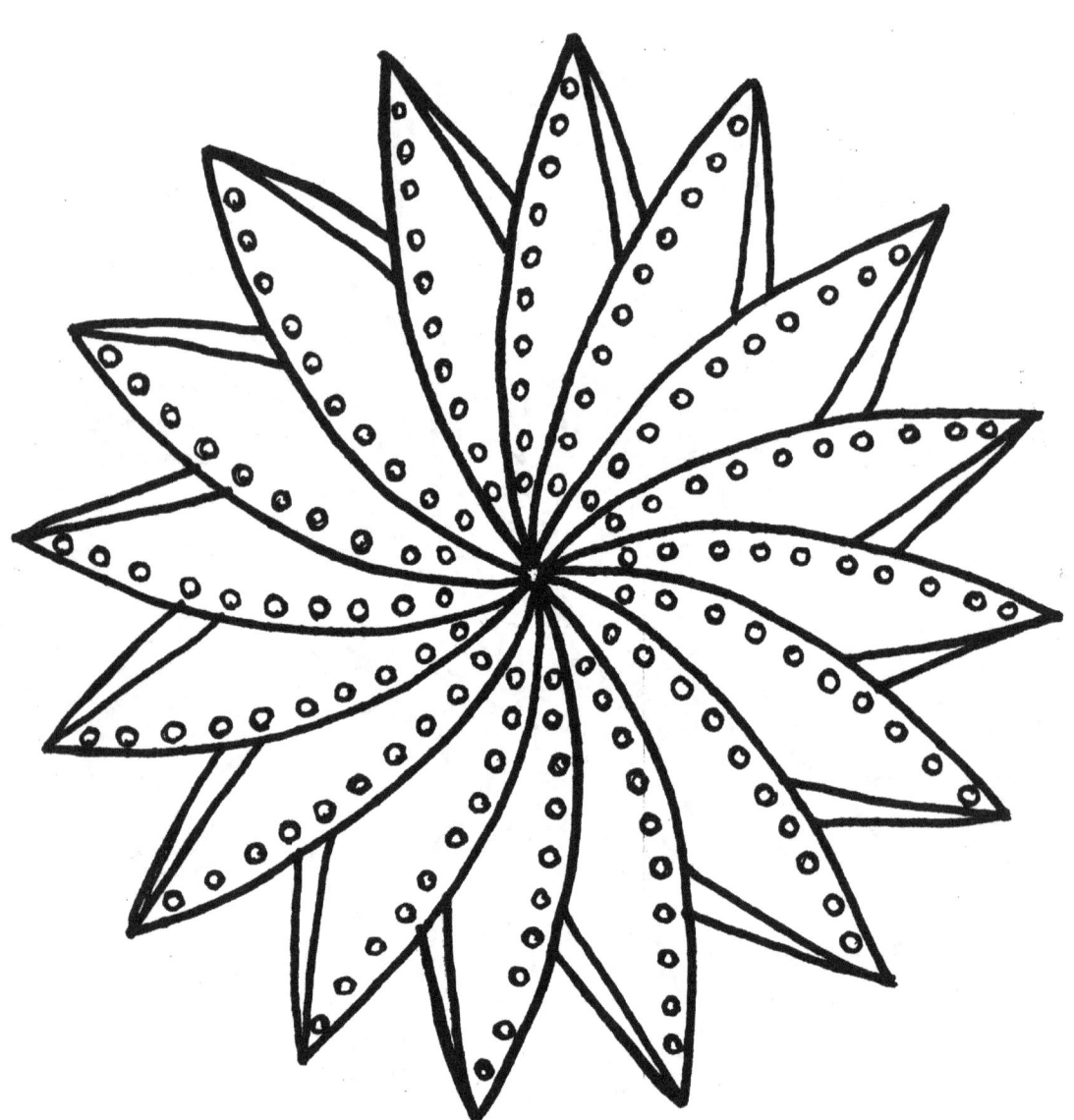

Copyright 2016

Christine Hardy

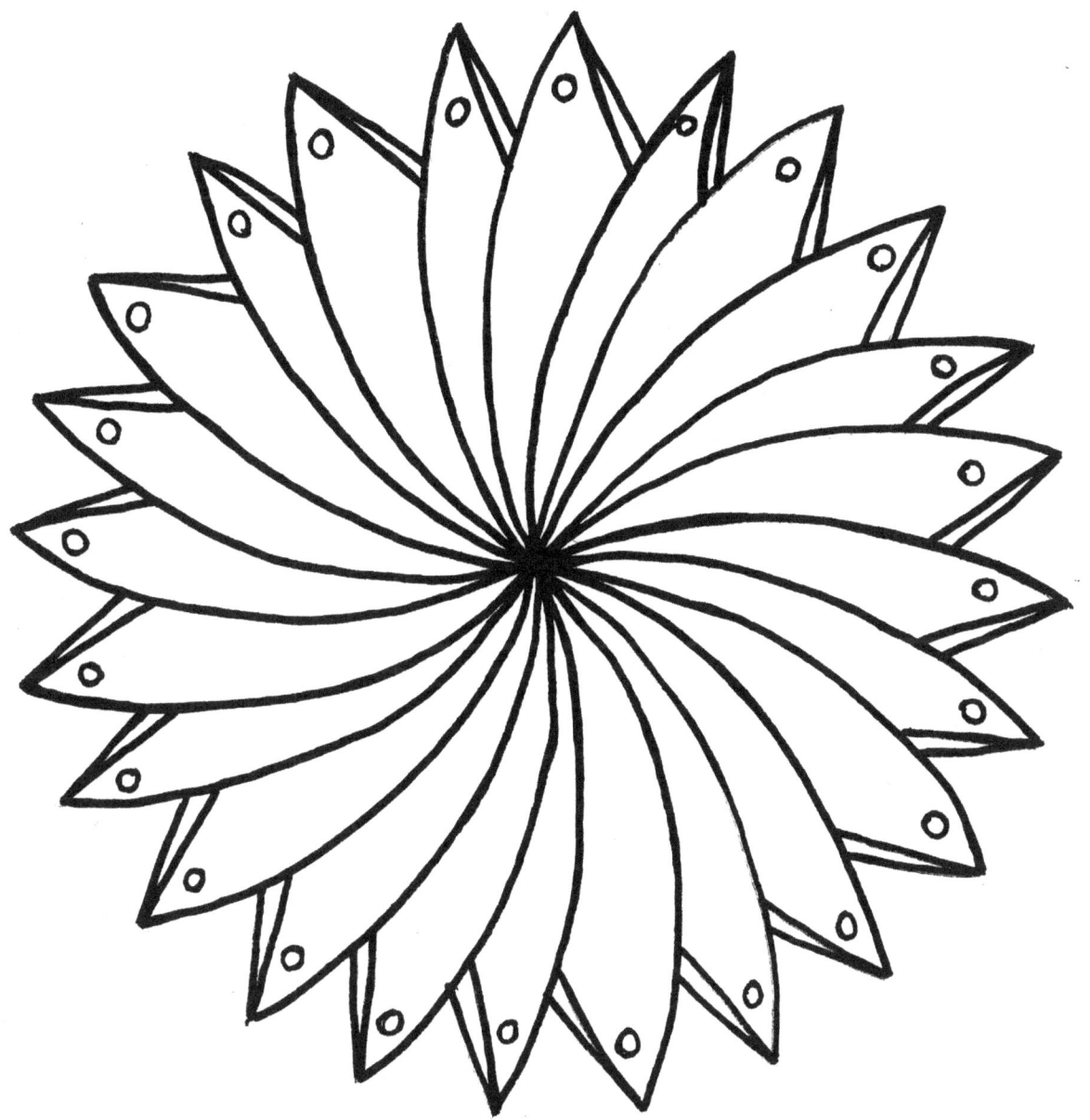

Copyright 2016

Christine Hardy

http://mycoloringbooks.info

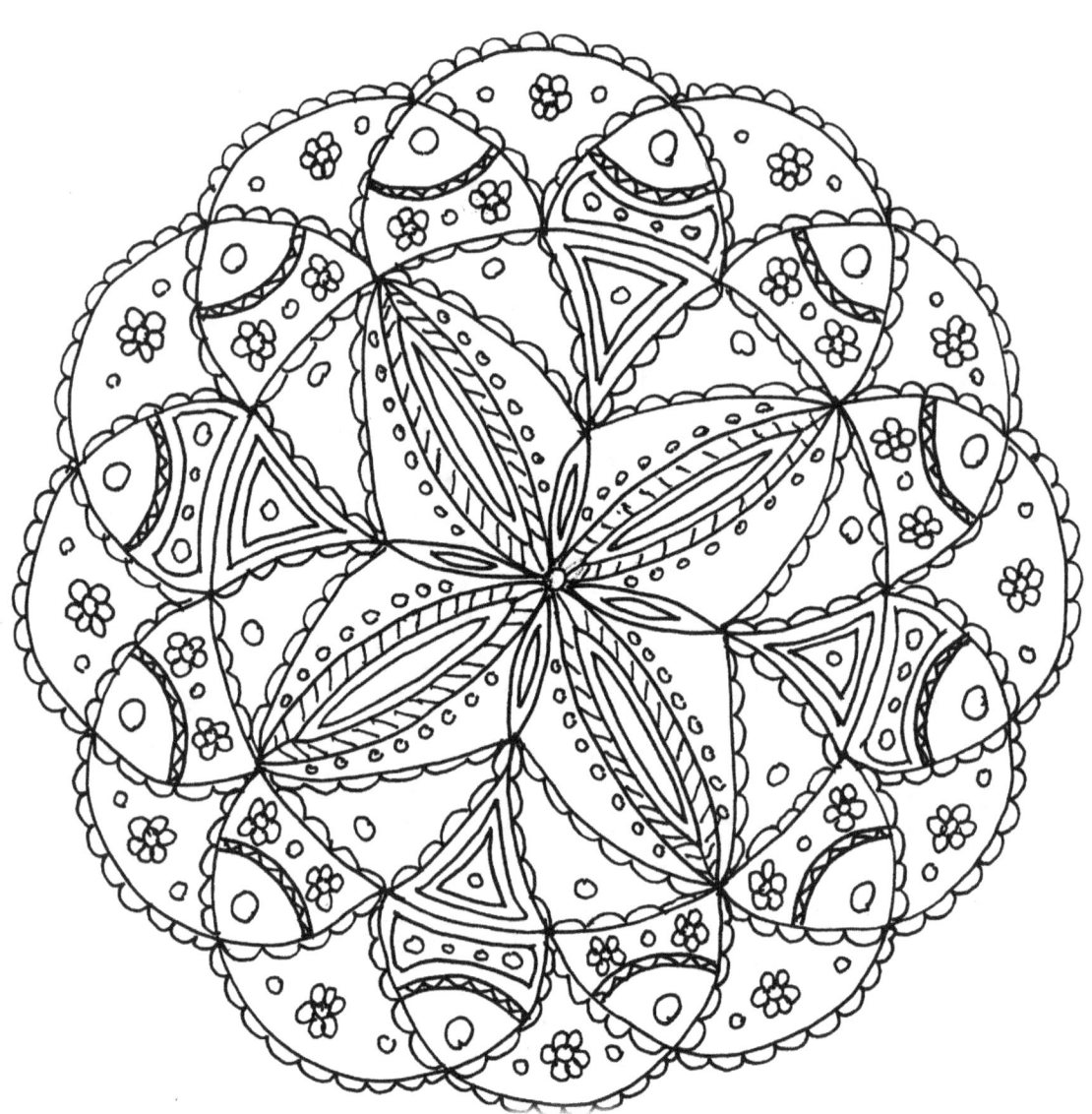

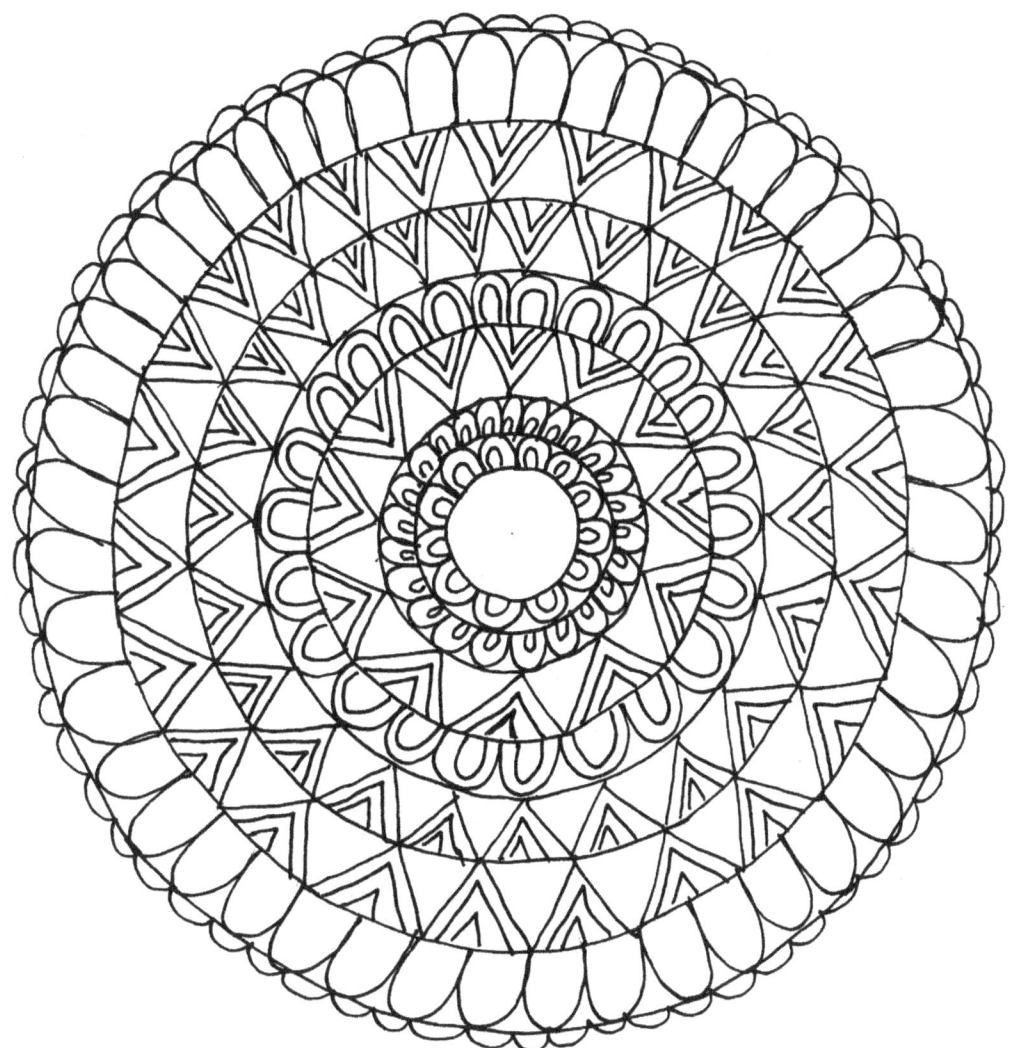

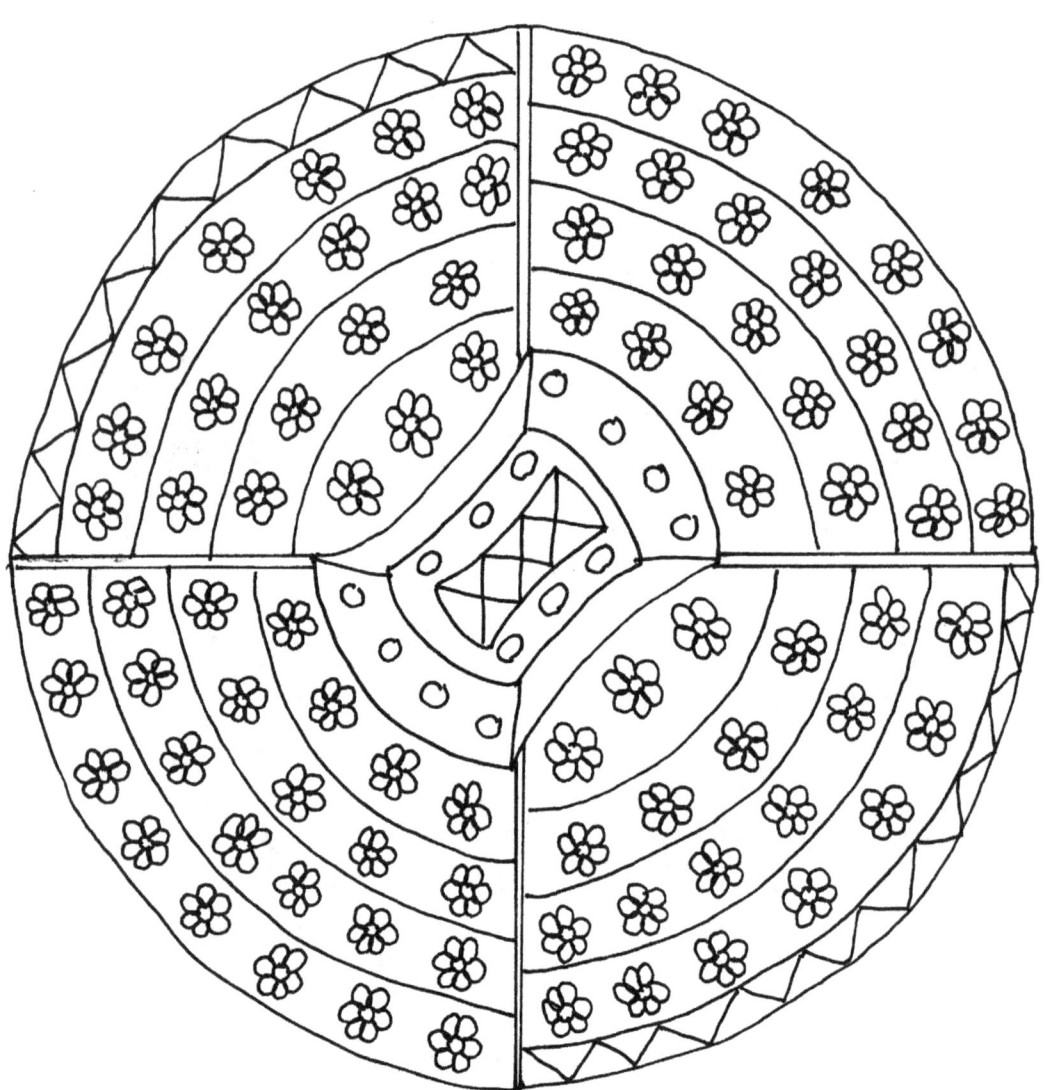

Copyright 2016

Christine Hardy

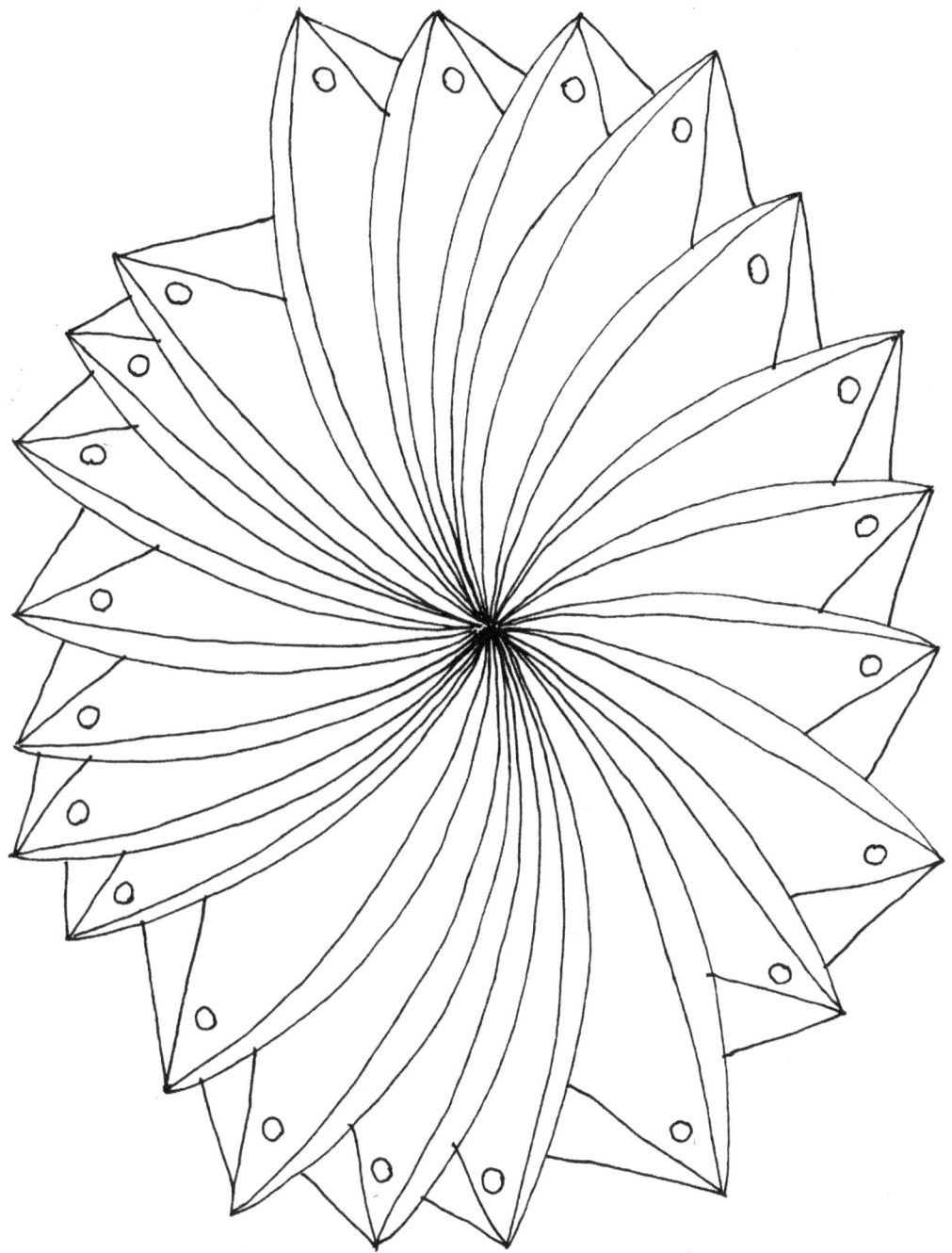

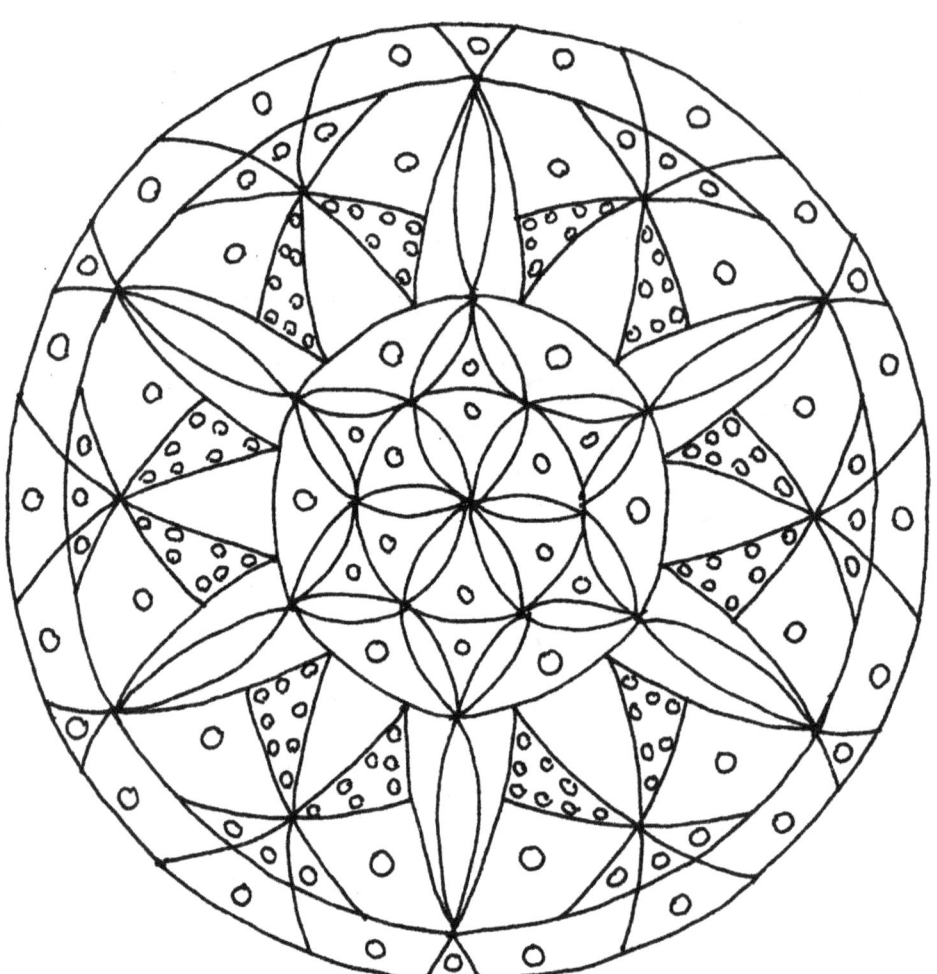

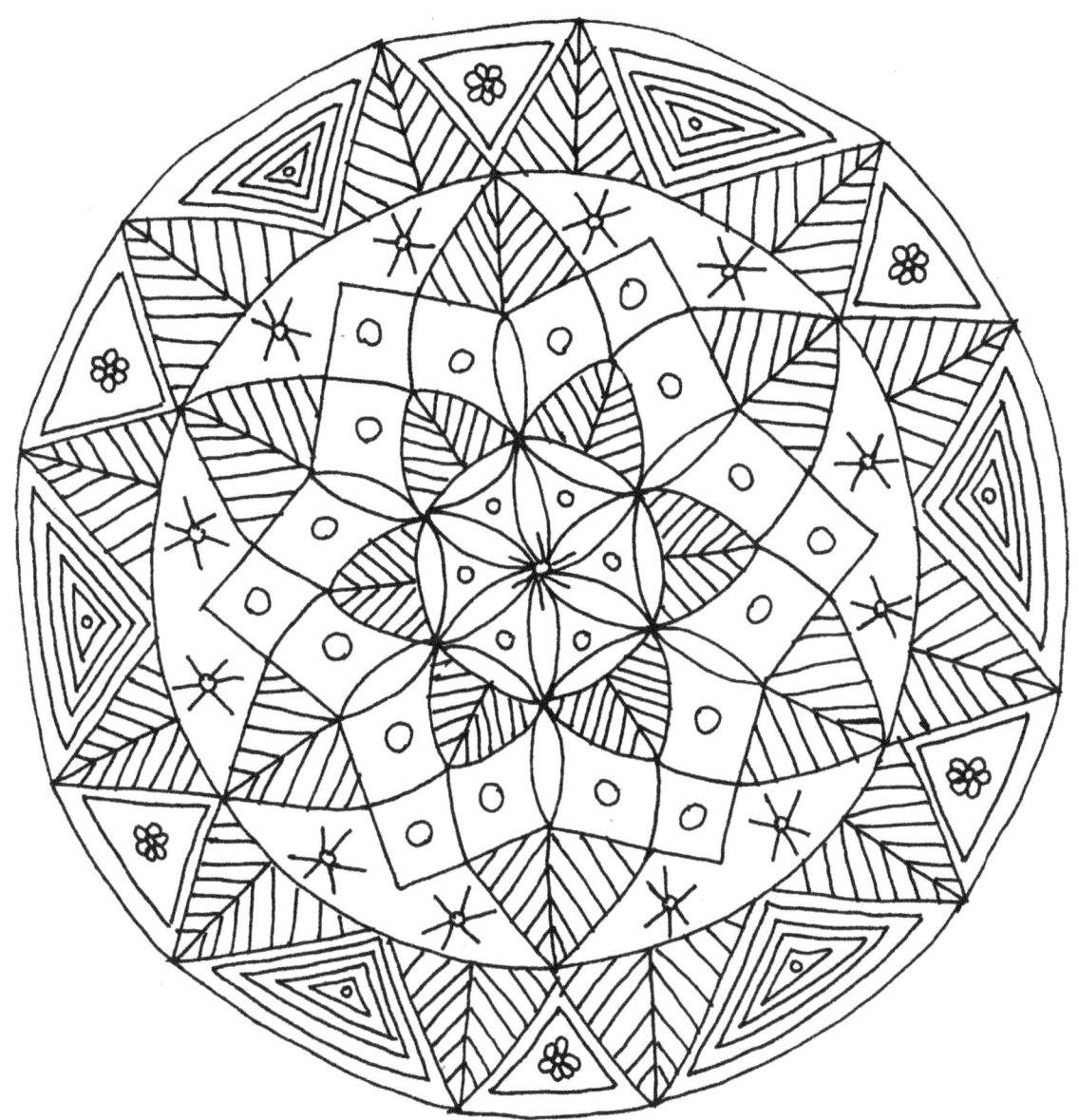

Copyright 2016

Christine Hardy

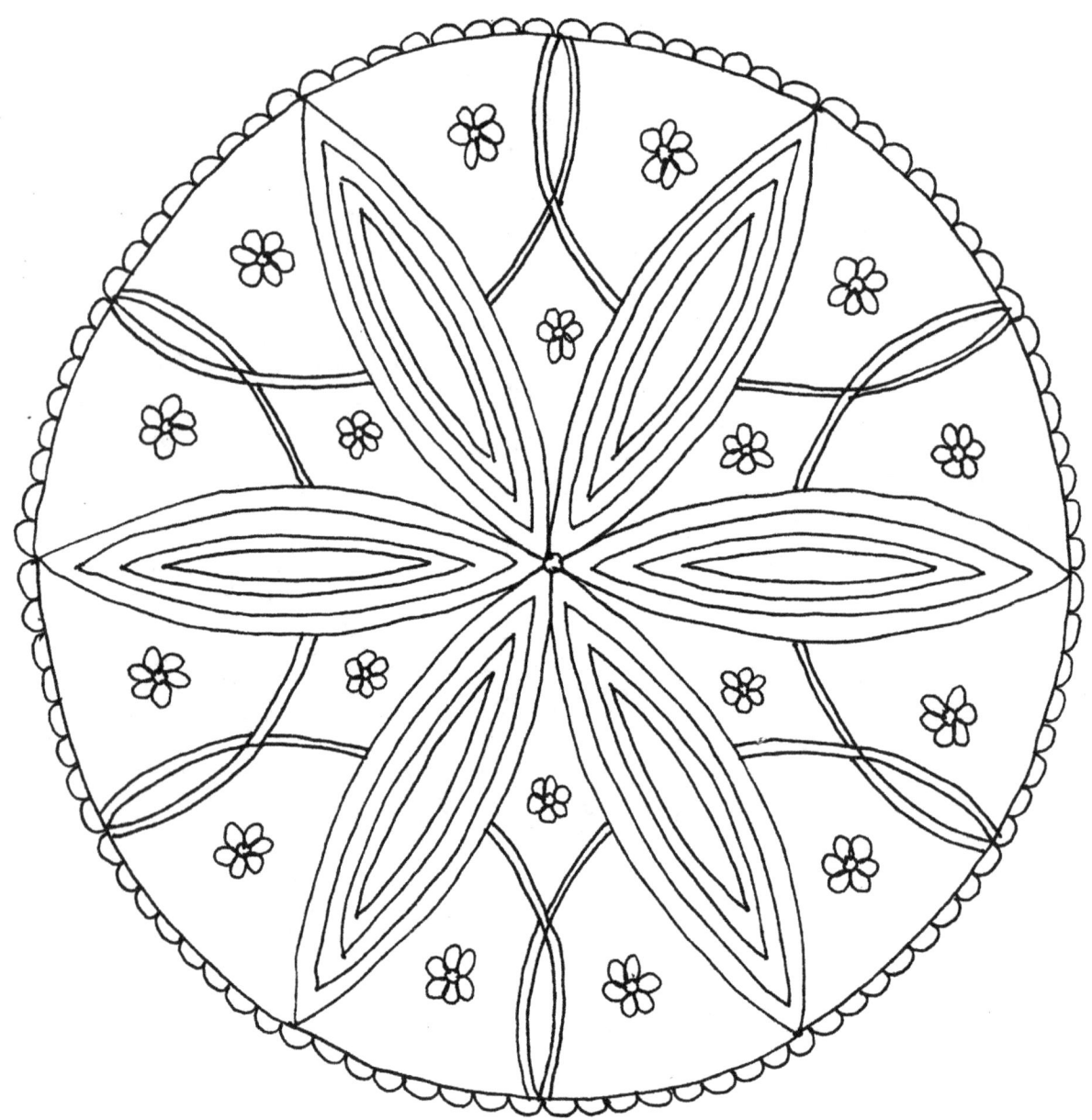

Copyright 2016

Christine Hardy

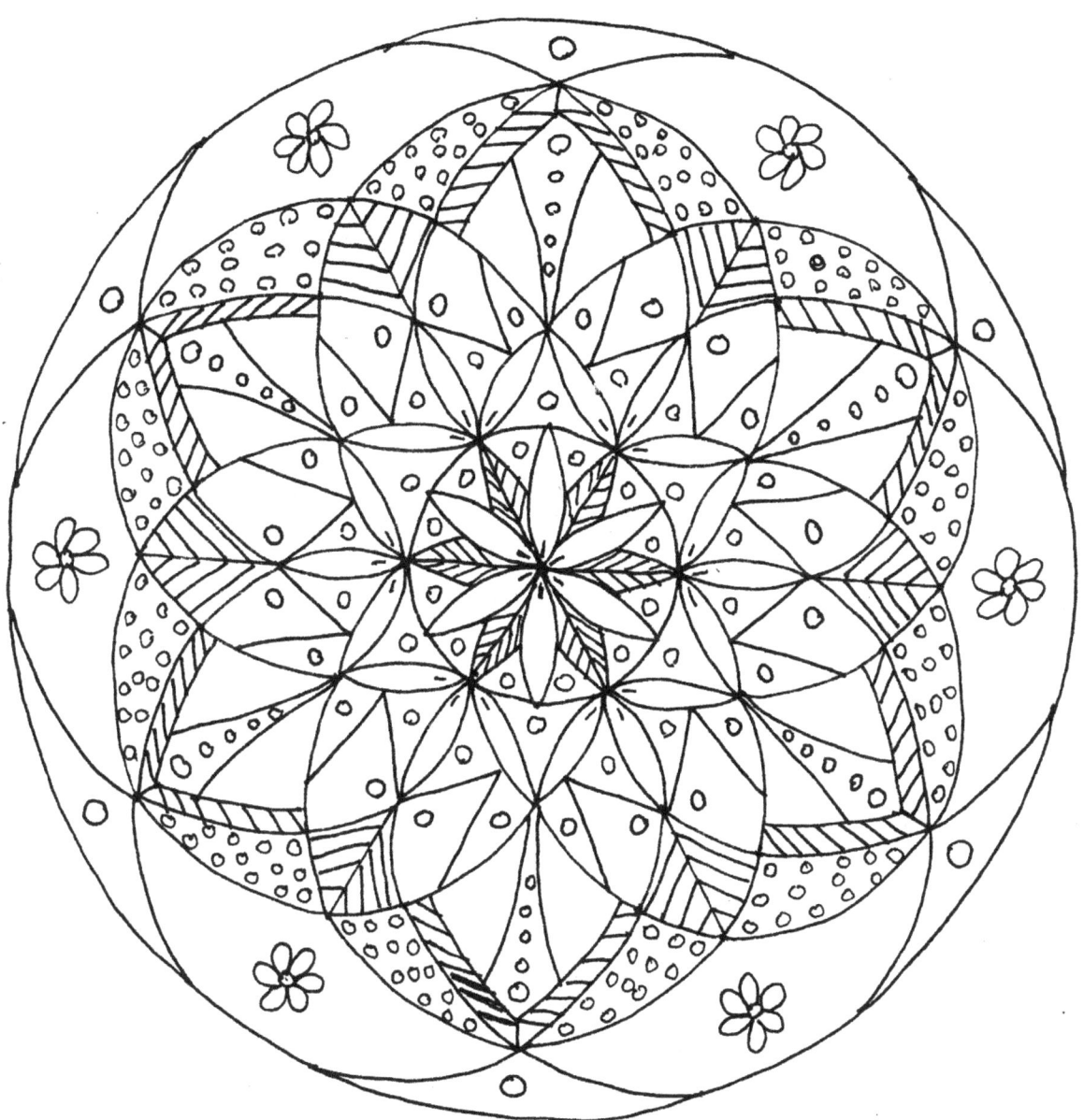

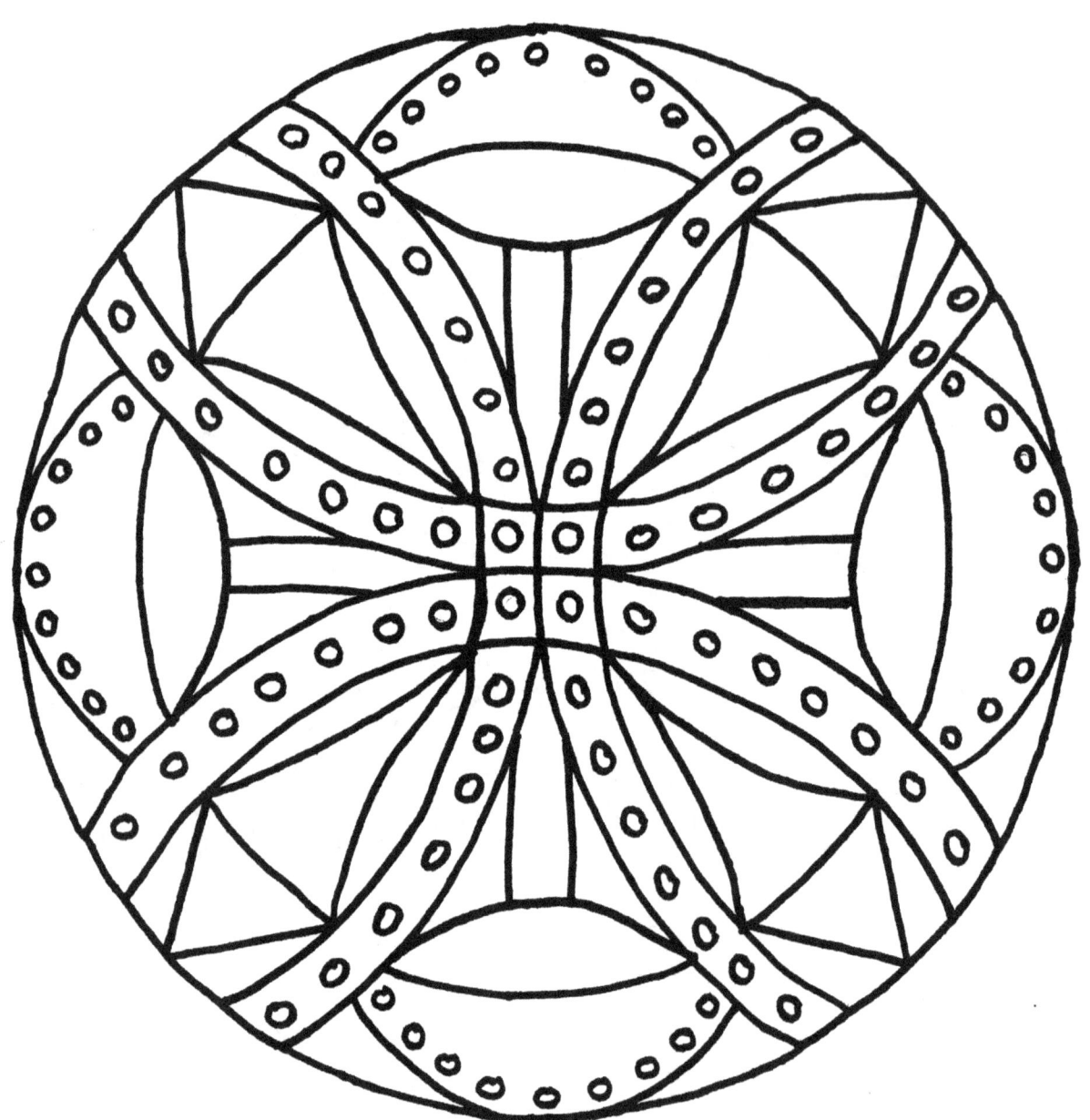

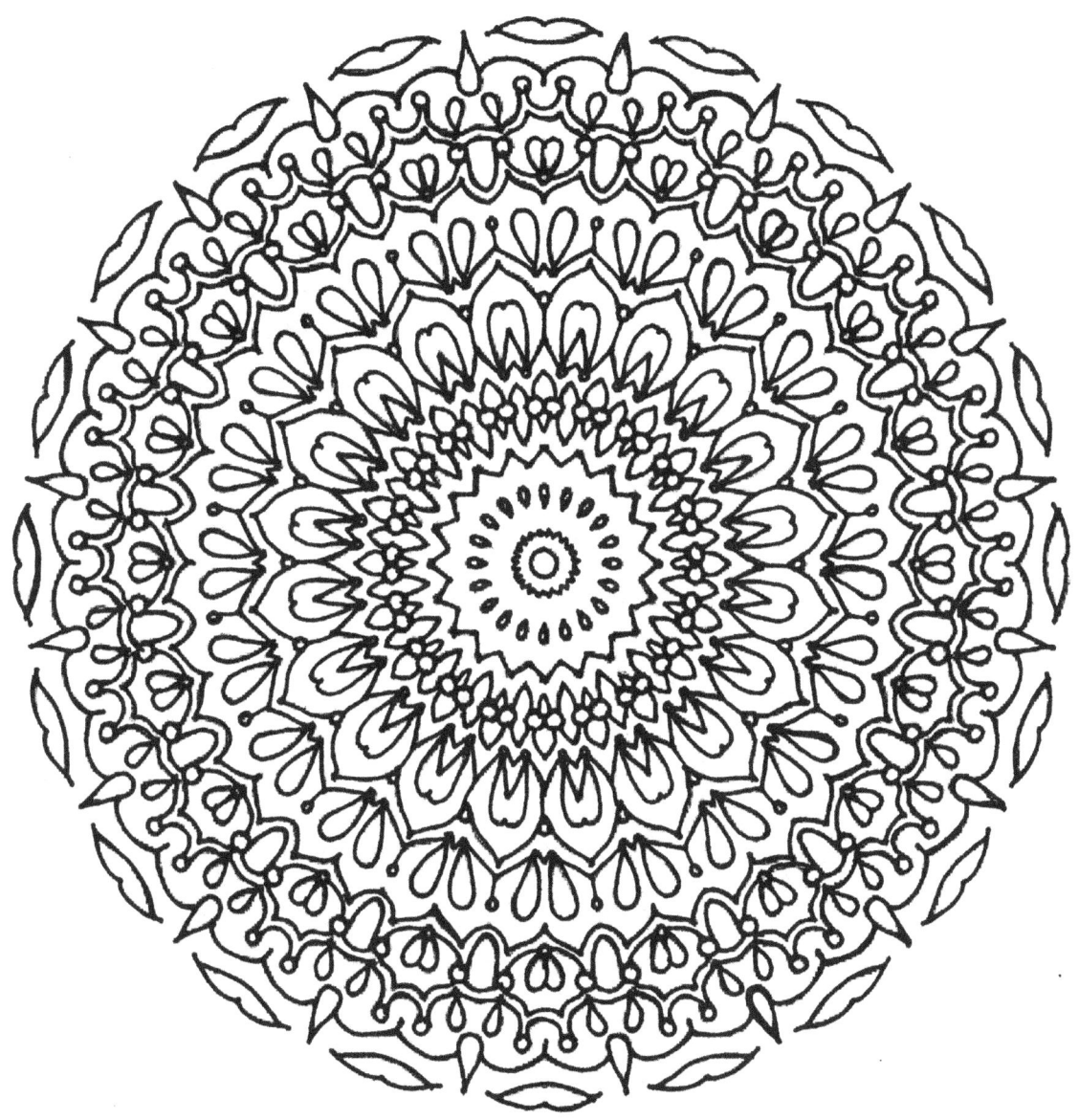

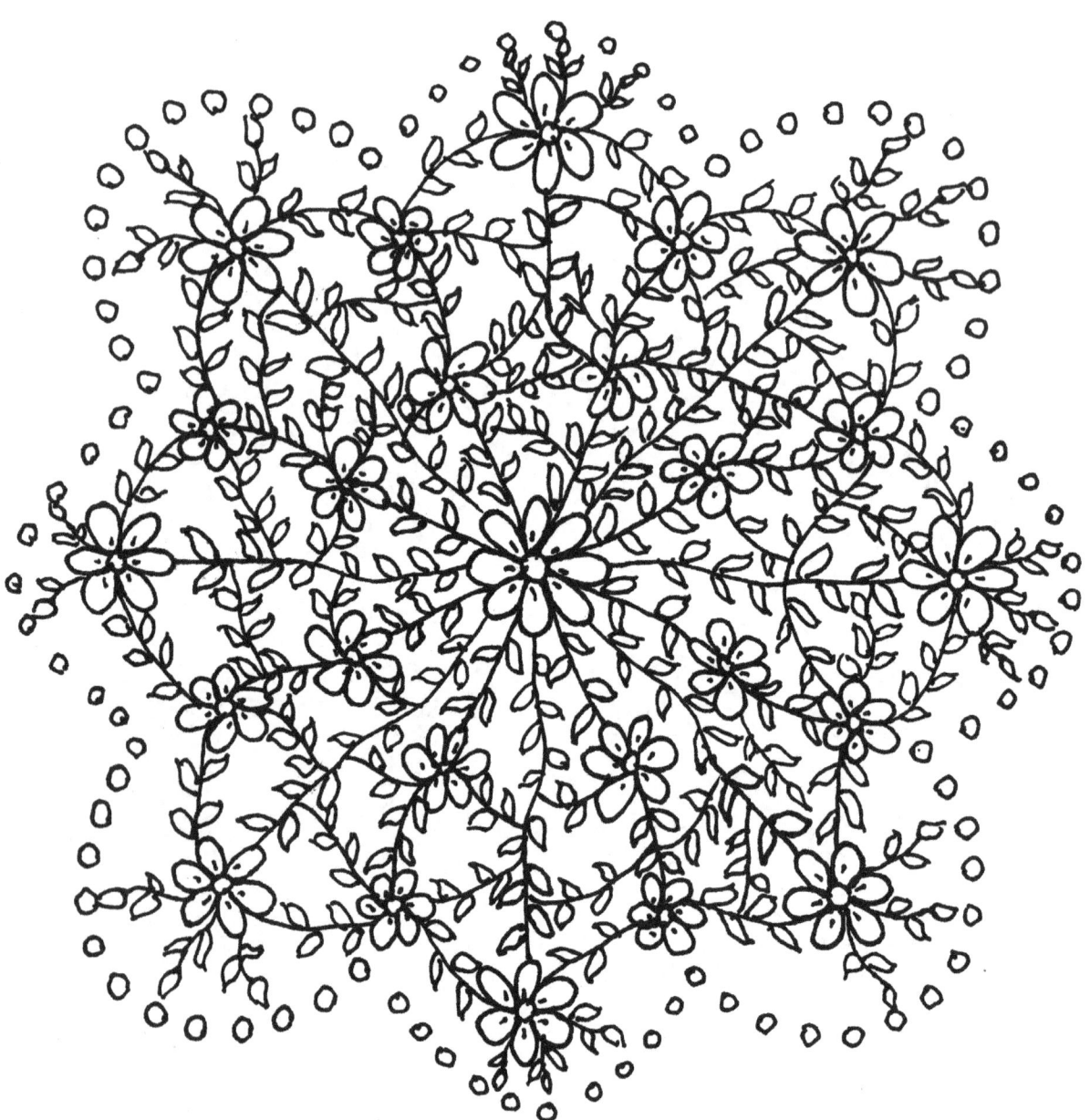

Copyright 2016

Christine Hardy

http://mycoloringbooks.info

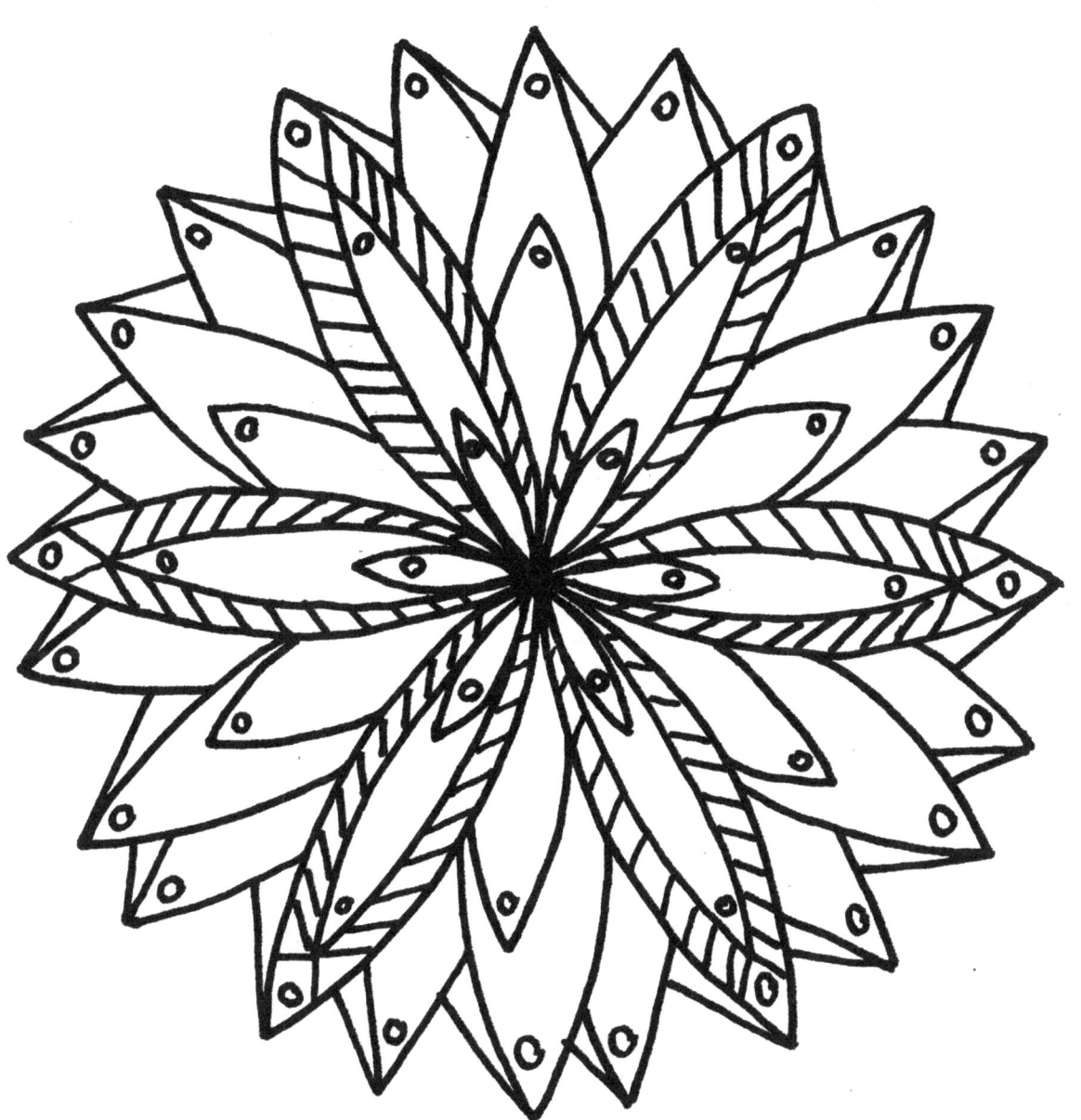

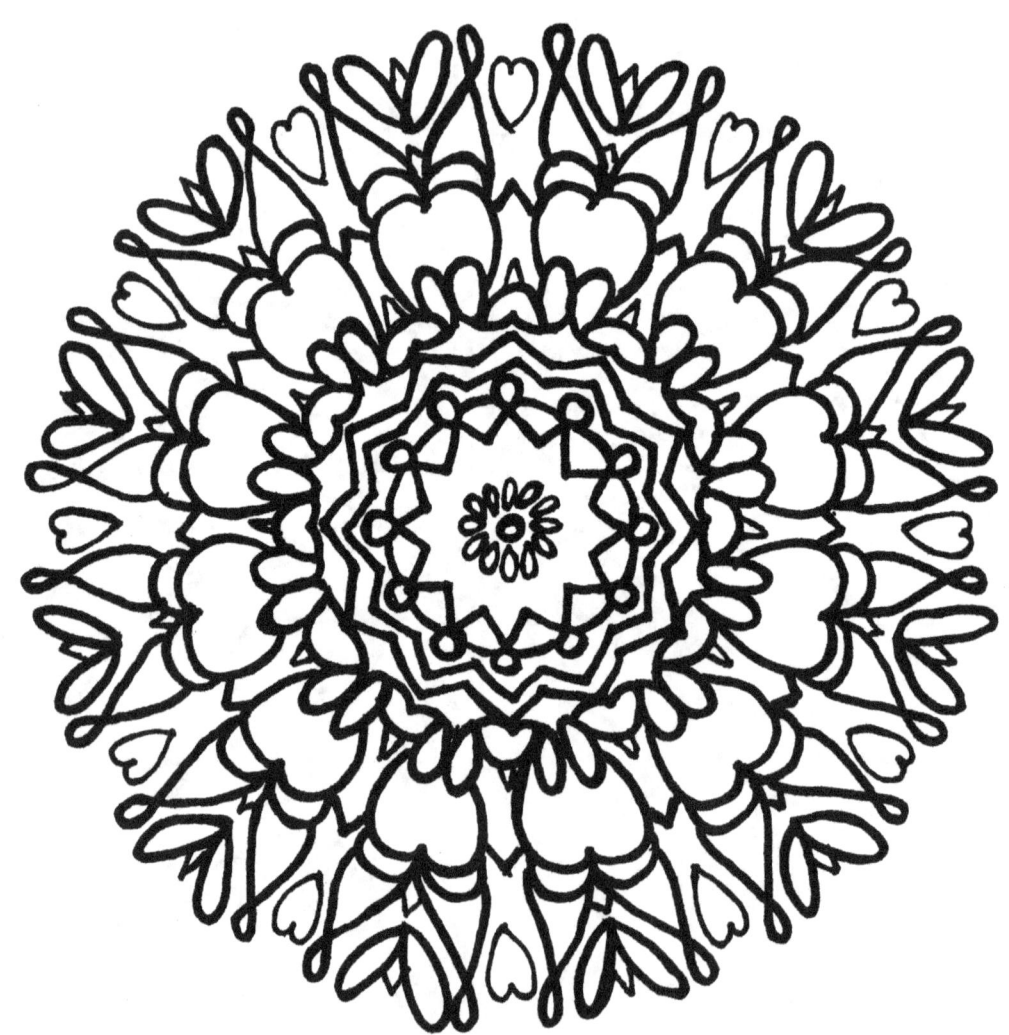

Copyright 2016

Christine Hardy

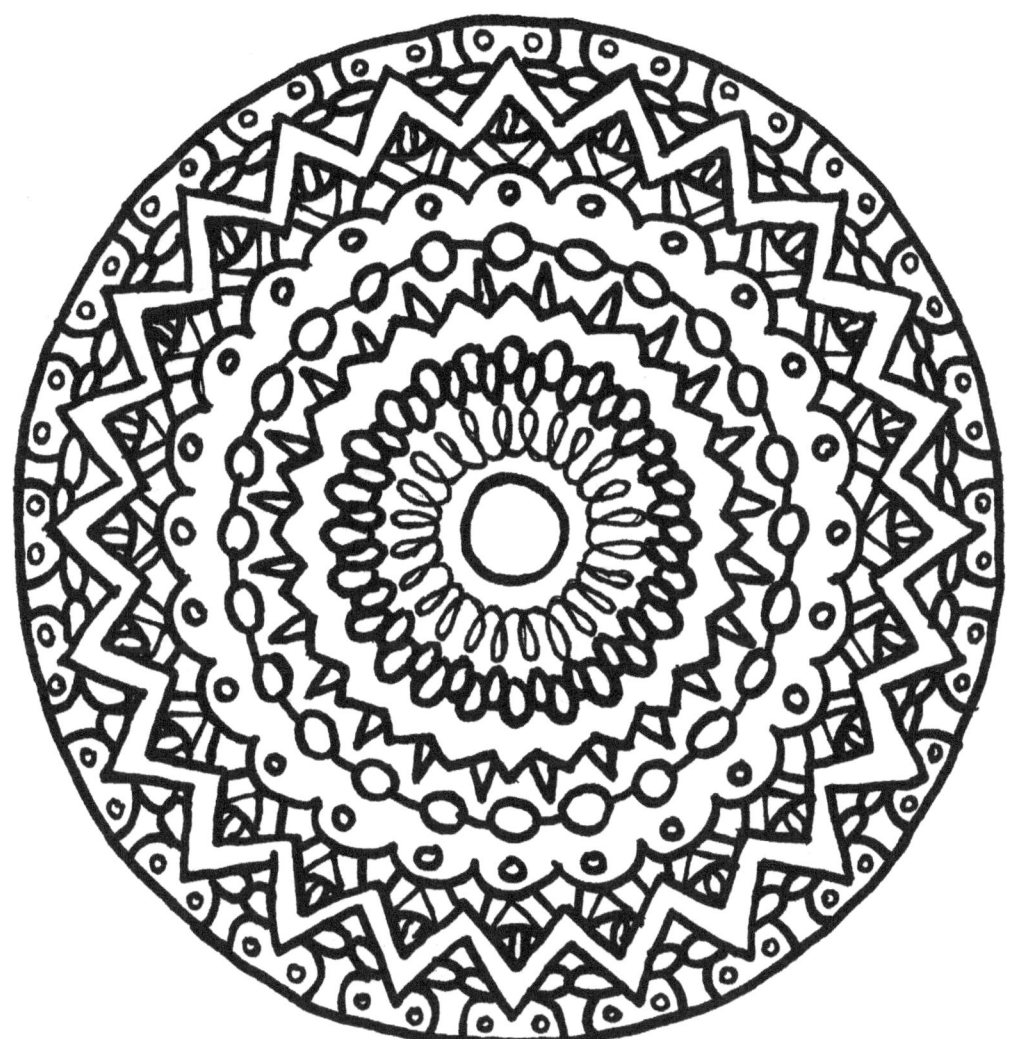

Christine Hardy

http://mycoloringbooks.info

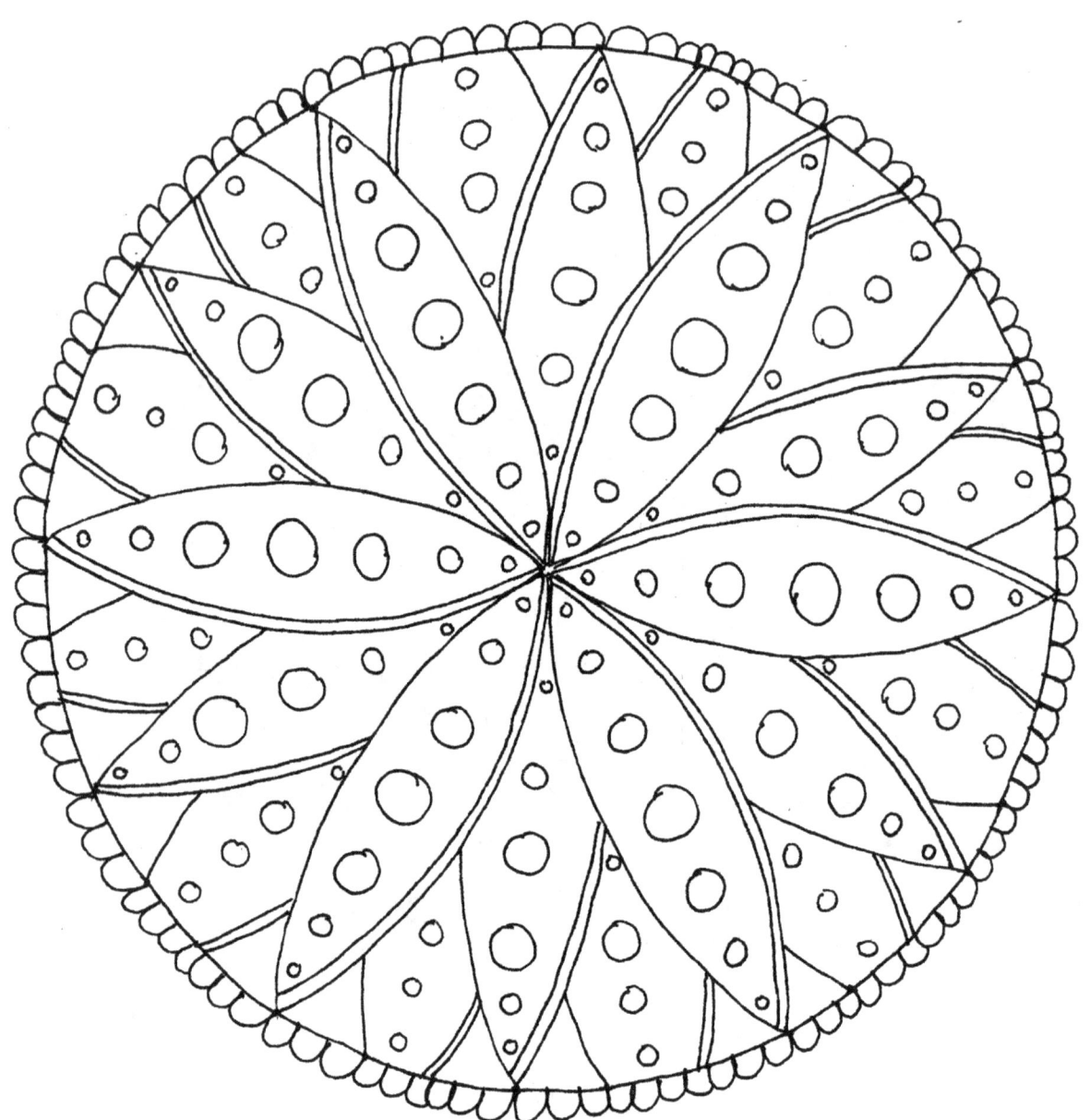

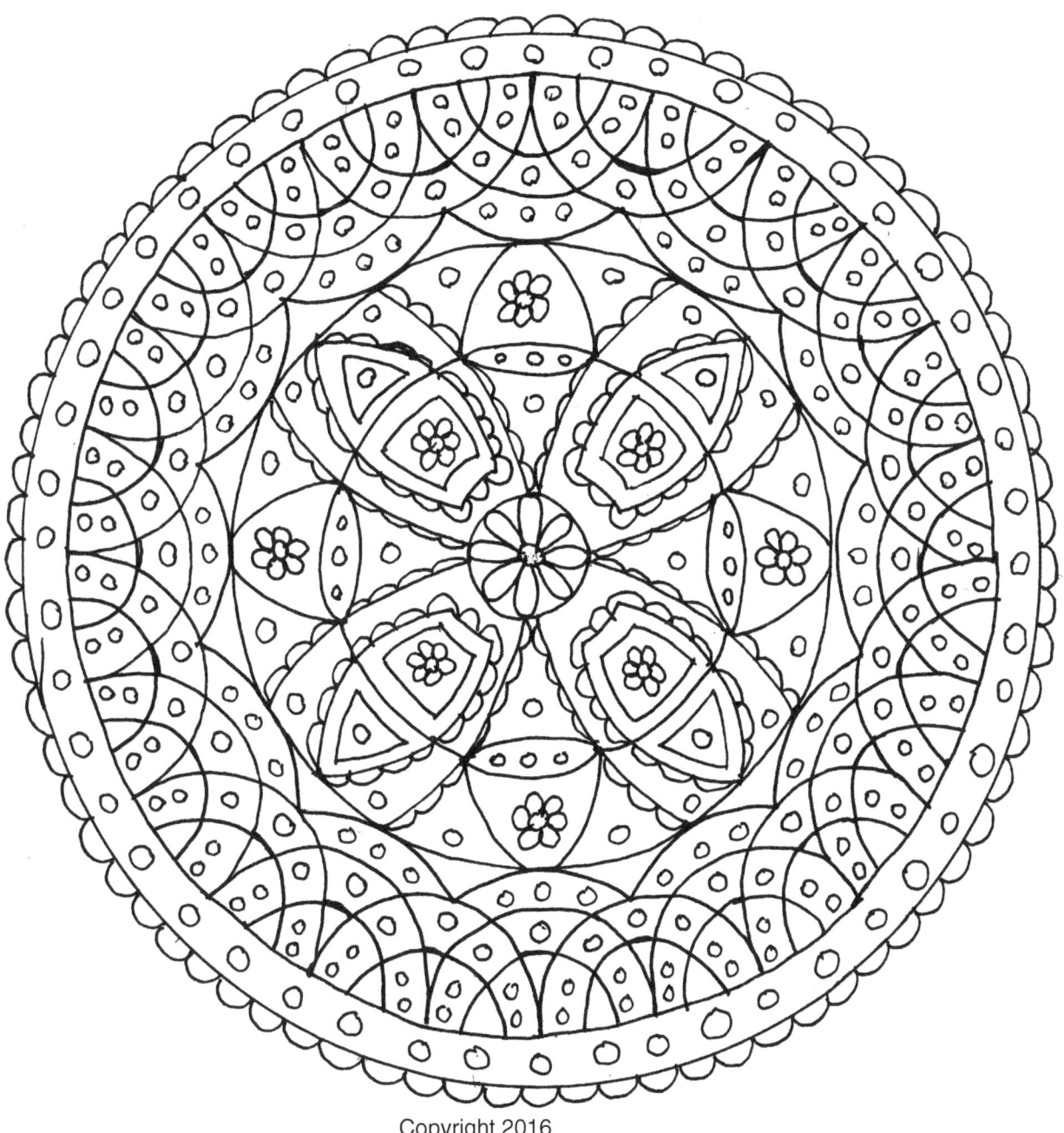

Copyright 2016
Christine Hardy

http://mycoloringbooks.info

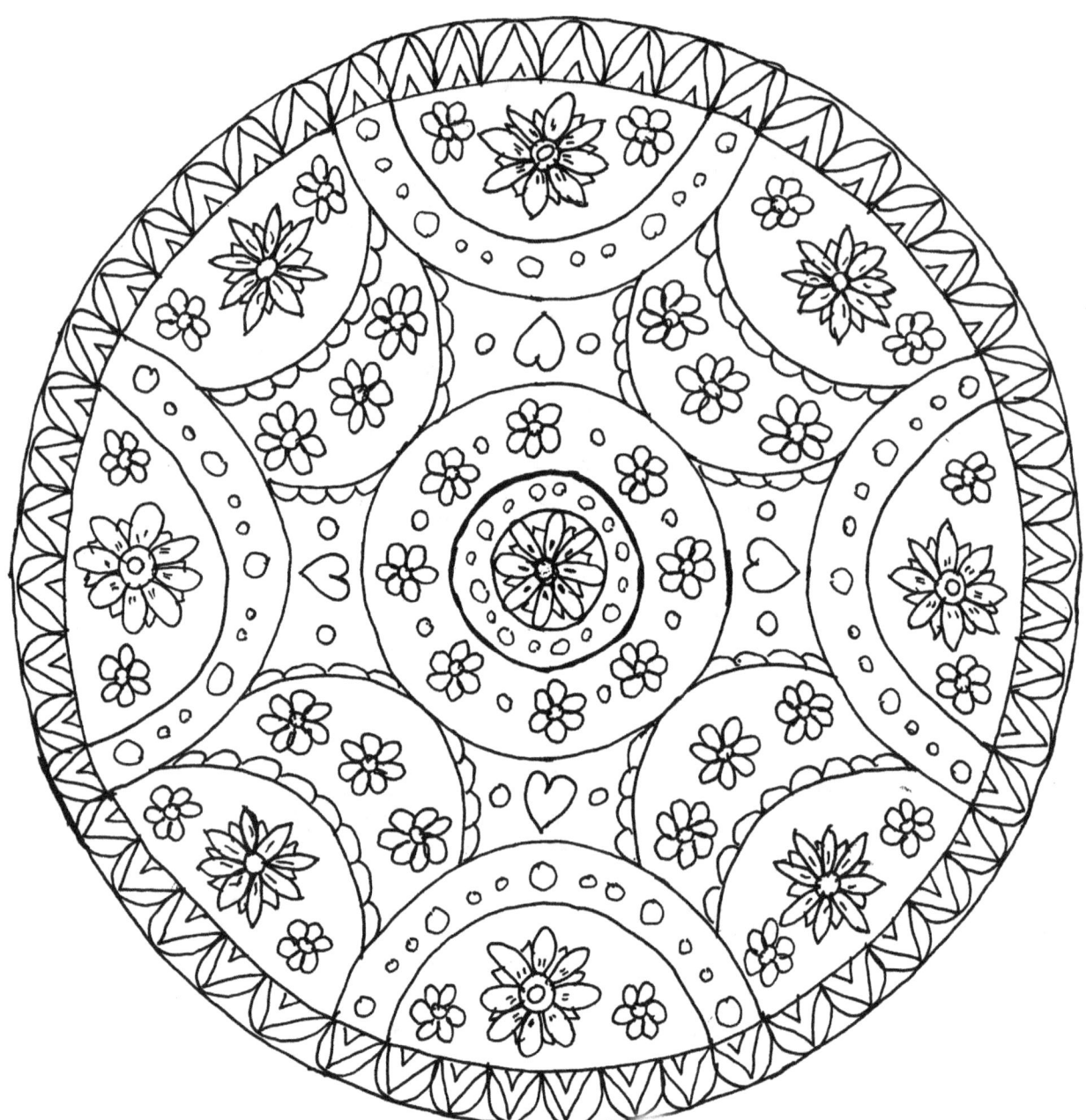

www.ingramcontent.com/pod-product-compliance
Lightning Source LLC
Chambersburg PA
CBHW080645190526
45169CB00009B/3516